classic themes by the masters

Arranged for Piano by James Bastien

PREFACE

CLASSIC THEMES BY THE MASTERS is designed to supplement THE OLDER BEGINNER PIANO COURSE, LEVEL 1. However, this volume may be used as supplementary enrichment with any piano course. The arrangements are accessible to the beginning pianist, and the timeless appeal of these well-known themes will provide hours of enjoyment for the pianist and listener.

Suggested Use of Materials with THE OLDER BEGINNER PIANO COURSE, LEVEL 1

When the student reaches **page 5**, he is ready to begin	Musicianship, Level 1 (WP34)
When the student reaches **page 14**, he is ready to begin	Music Flashcards (GP27)
When the student reaches **page 15**, he is ready to begin	Notespeller, Level 1 (WP20)
When the student reaches **page 44**, he is ready to begin	Classic Themes by the Masters (WP40)
When the student reaches **page 46**, he is ready to begin	Religious Favorites (WP41)
When the student reaches **page 48**, he is ready to begin	Favorite Melodies the World Over, Level 1 (WP37)
When the student reaches **page 53**, he is ready to begin	Pop, Rock 'N Blues, Book 1 (GP37)

© 1978, 1980
℗ 1978 Kjos West, San Diego, California
Any reproduction, adaptation or arrangement of this work in whole or in part without the consent of the copyright owner constitutes an infringement of copyright.
All Rights Reserved. International Copyright Secured. Printed in U.S.A.

Published by Kjos West.
National Order Desk, 4382 Jutland Dr., San Diego, CA 92117

ISBN 0-8497-5037-7

The Bastien Older Beginner Piano Library

Contents

Composer Index

4

MORNING MOOD

from "Peer Gynt Suite," No. 1, Op. 46
(Theme from 1st Movement)

EDVARD GREIG

arranged by James Bastien

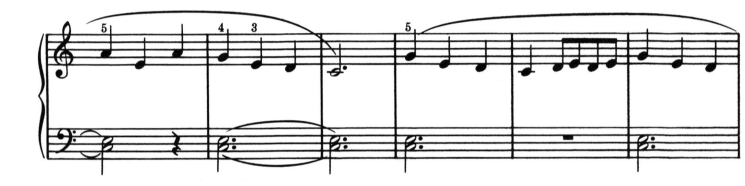

WP40

ODE TO JOY
from the Symphony No. 9, Op. 125
(Theme from 4th Movement)

LUDWIG VAN BEETHOVEN
arranged by James Bastien

Spiritoso

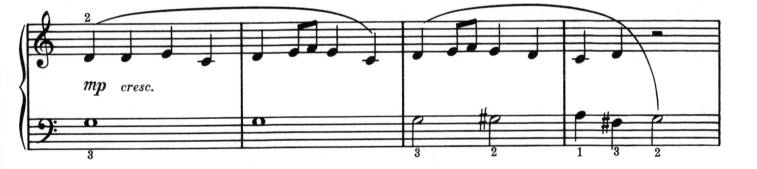

ON WINGS OF SONG

from Op. 34, No. 2 for voice and piano

FELIX MENDELSSOHN
arranged by James Bastien

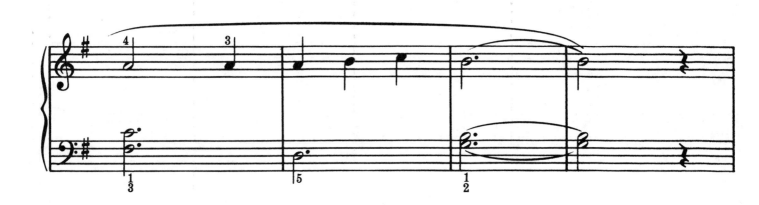

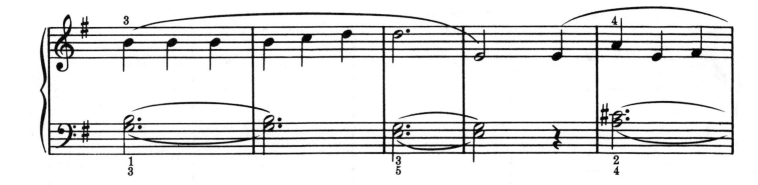

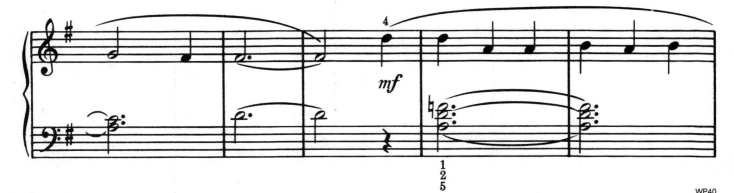

WP40

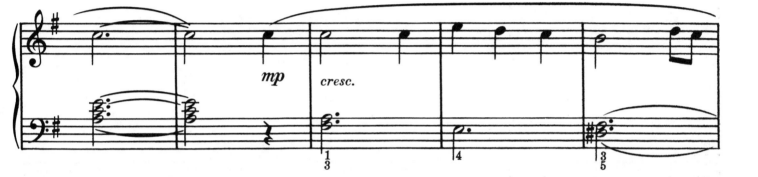

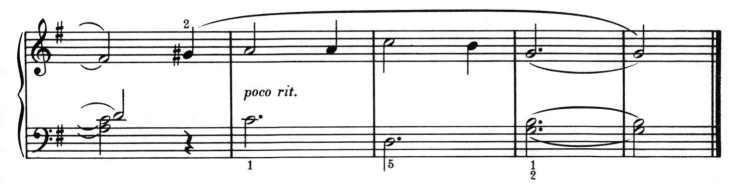

ARIA

from the opera "Marriage of Figaro," Act I

WOLFGANG AMADEUS MOZART

arranged by James Bastien

Moderato

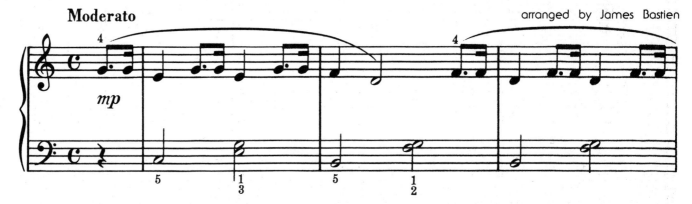

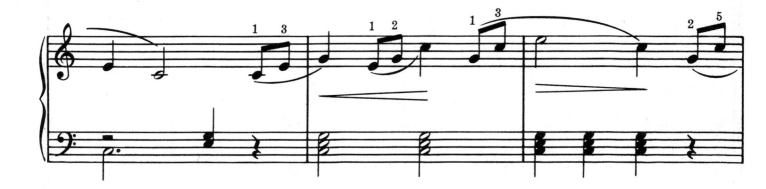

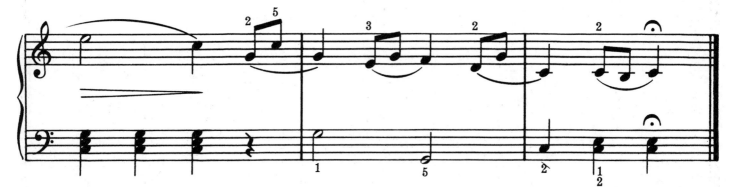

MARCH MILITAIRE

from Op. 51, No. 1 for piano, four hands
(1st Theme)

FRANZ SCHUBERT

arranged by James Bastien

Tempo di marcia

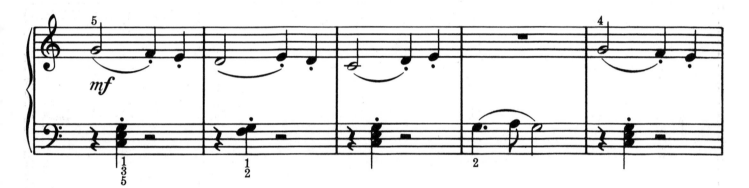

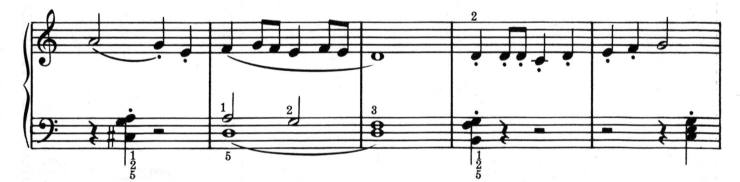

WP40

LULLABY

from "Wiegenlied" ("Cradle Song"), Op. 49, No. 4 for voice and piano

JOHANNES BRAHMS

arranged by James Bastien

Andante

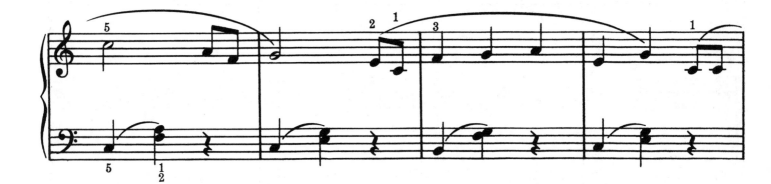

WP40

HALLELUJAH CHORUS

from the oratorio "Messiah" for solo voices, chorus, and orchestra

GEORGE FREDERIC HANDEL

arranged by James Bastien

Allegro maestoso

THE BLUE DANUBE

from the Concert Waltz Op. 314

JOHANN STRAUSS, JR.

arranged by James Bastien

Tempo di valse

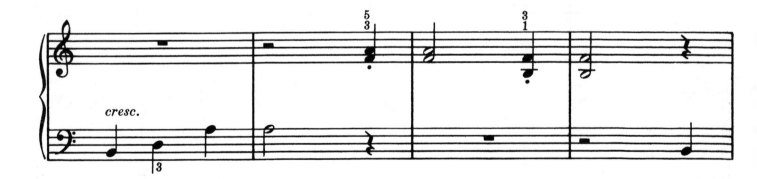

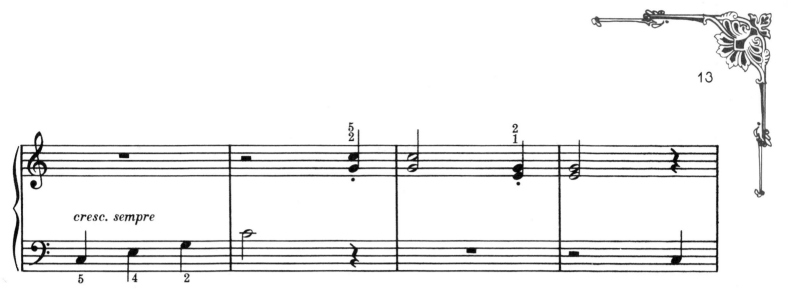

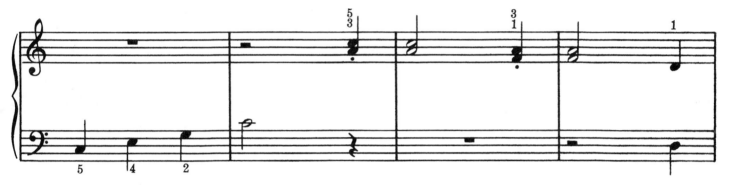

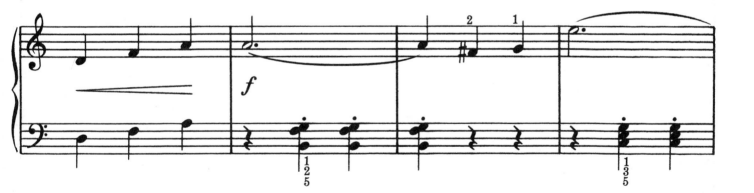

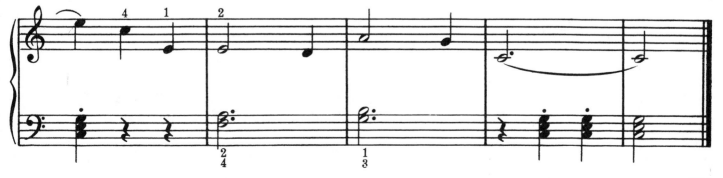

BOURRÉE

from the Partita No. 1 for violin

JOHANN SEBASTIAN BACH

arranged by James Bastien

Allegro moderato

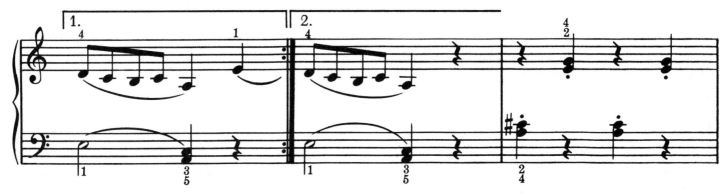

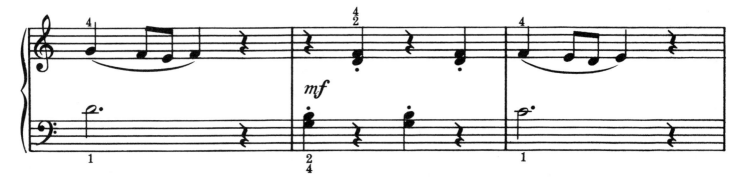

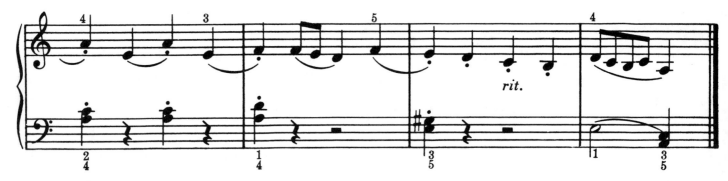

WP40

FÜR ELISE

from the Bagatelle Op. 173 for piano

LUDWIG VAN BEETHOVEN

arranged by James Bastien

Allegretto

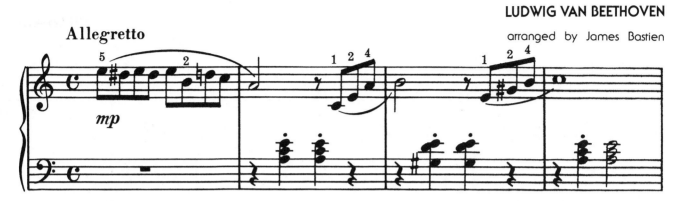

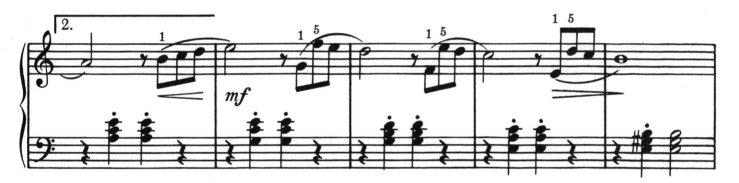

"PATHETIQUE" SYMPHONY

from the Symphony No. 6, Op. 74
(Theme from 1st Movement)

PETER ILYICH TCHAIKOVSKY

arranged by James Bastien

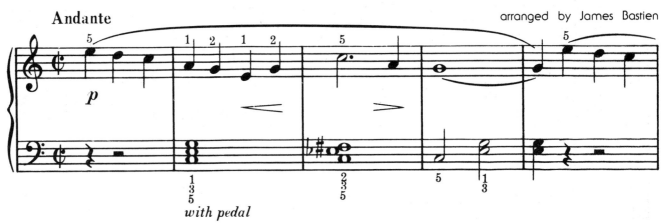

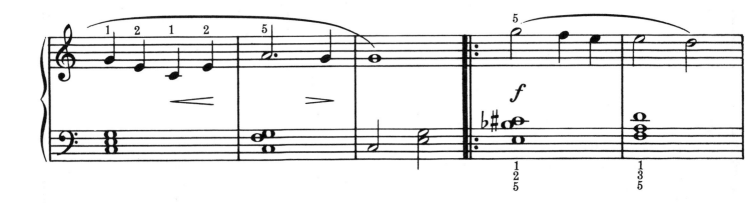

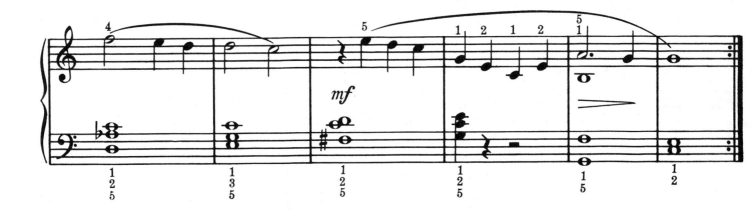

WP4

LARGO

from the Symphony No. 5, Op. 95 ("From the New World")
(Theme from 2nd Movement)

ANTONIN DVOŘÁK

arranged by James Bastien

Largo

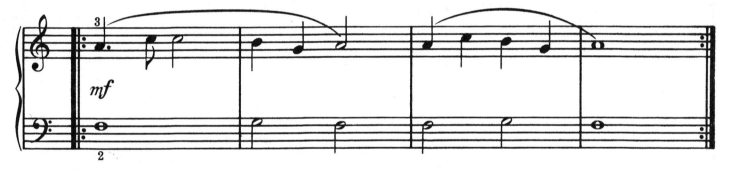

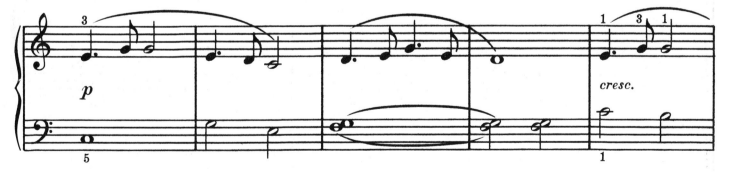

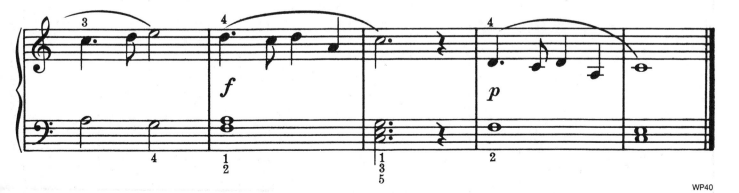

"SURPRISE" SYMPHONY

from the Symphony in G, No. 94, Op. 80, No. 1
(Theme from 2nd Movement)

FRANZ JOSEPH HAYDN

arranged by James Bastien

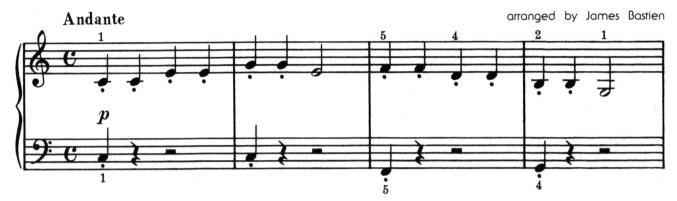

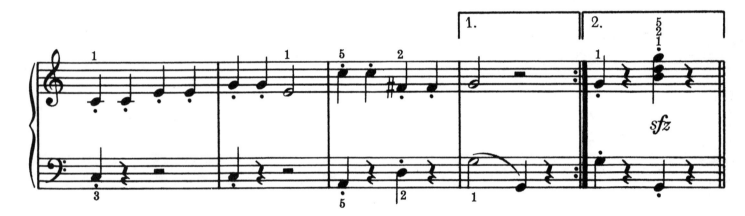

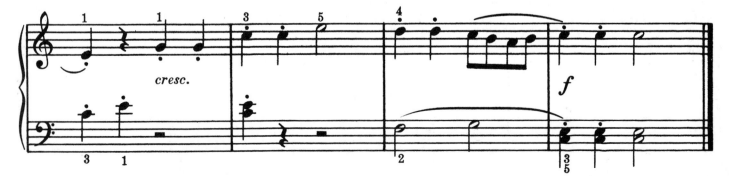

WP40

WEDDING MARCH

from "A Midsummer Night's Dream," Op. 61, No. 9 for voice, chorus, and orchestra

FELIX MENDELSSOHN

arranged by James Bastien

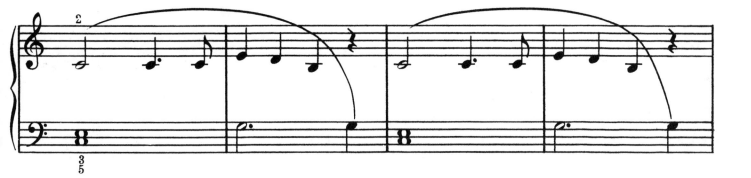

SYMPHONY IN D MINOR
(Theme from 2nd Movement)

CÉSAR FRANCK

arranged by James Bastien

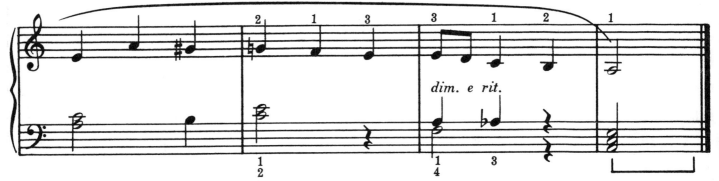

WP40

FANTASIE-IMPROMPTU

from the Impromptu Op. 66 for piano

(2nd Theme)

FRÉDÉRIC CHOPIN

arranged by James Bastien

Moderato cantabile

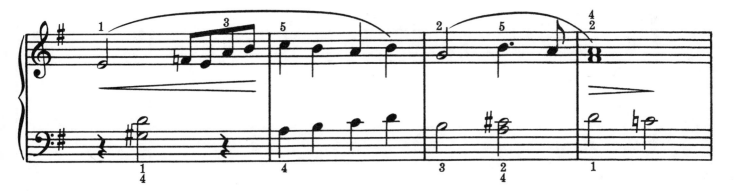

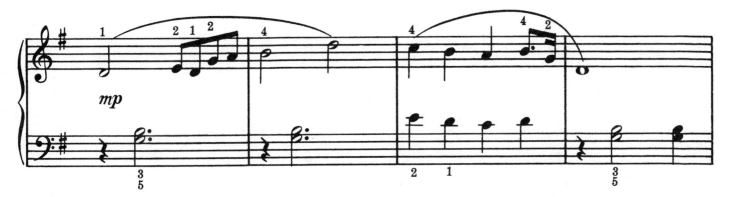

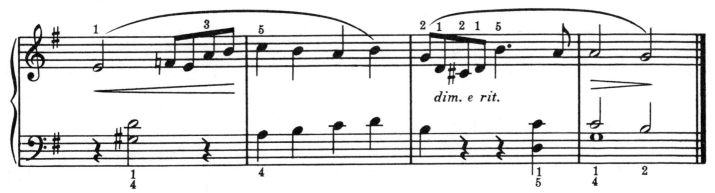

SICILIANA
from the Sonata No. 2 for flute and harpsichord

JOHANN SEBASTIAN BACH
arranged by James Bastien

Andantino

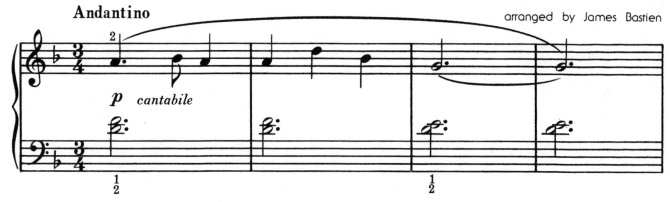

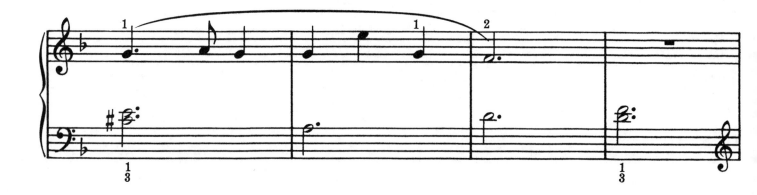

WP40

a tempo

dim. e rit.

SHEEP MAY SAFELY GRAZE

from the Cantata No. 208, No. 9 ("Birthday Cantata") for solo voices, chorus. and orchestra

JOHANN SEBASTIAN BACH

arranged by James Bastien

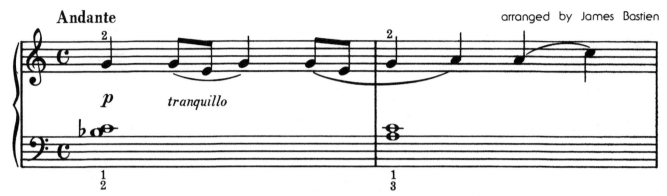

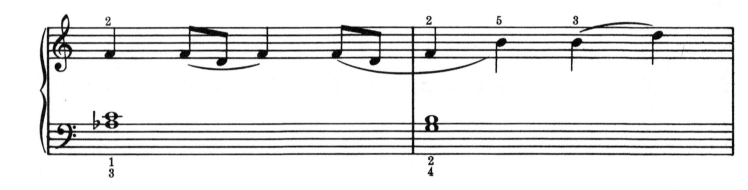

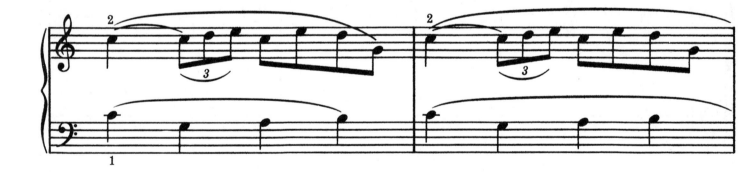

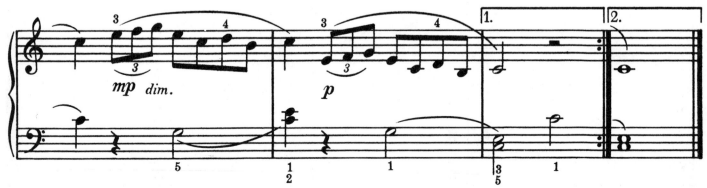

WP40

CAN-CAN
from the opera "Orpheus in the Underworld"

JACQUES OFFENBACH
arranged by James Bastien

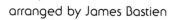

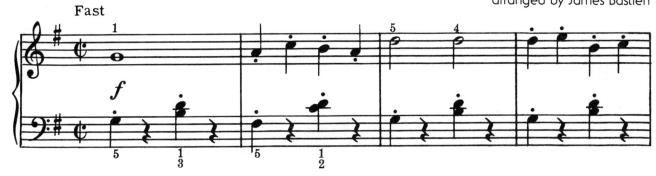

MELODY IN F
from Op. 3, No. 1 for piano

ANTON RUBINSTEIN

arranged by James Bastien

Moderato

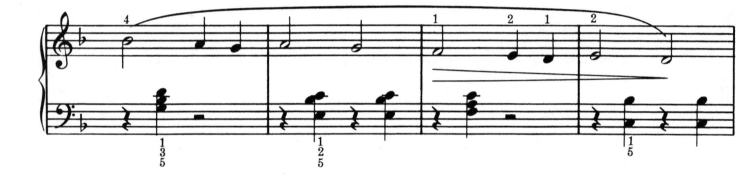

SYMPHONY NO. 1

from Op. 68
(Theme from 4th Movement)

JOHANNES BRAHMS

arranged by James Bastien

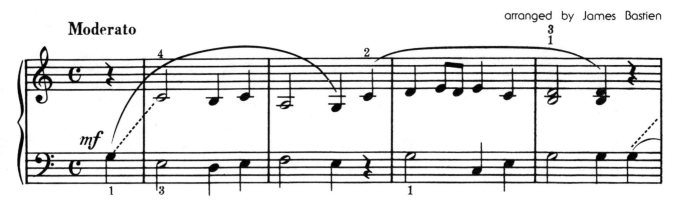

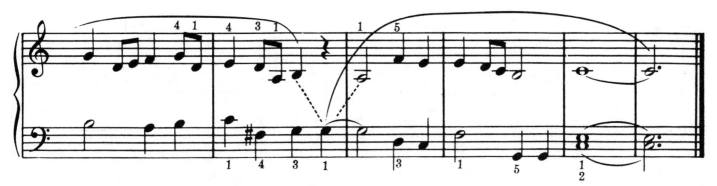

WP40

LA DONNA E MOBILE

from the opera "Rigoletto," Act III

GIUSEPPE VERDI

arranged by James Bastien

Con spirito

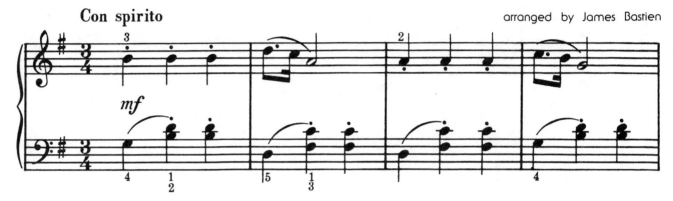

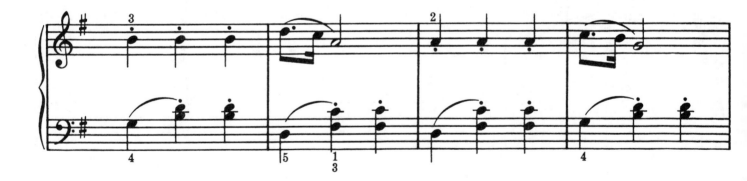

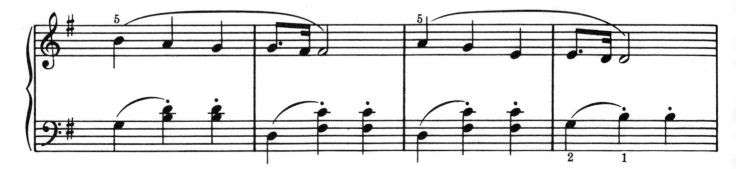

WP40

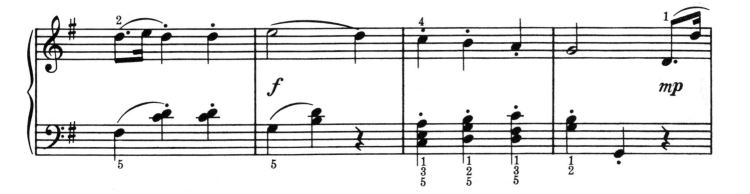

SWAN LAKE
Theme from the Ballet Op. 20

PETER ILYICH TCHAIKOVSKY

arranged by James Bastien

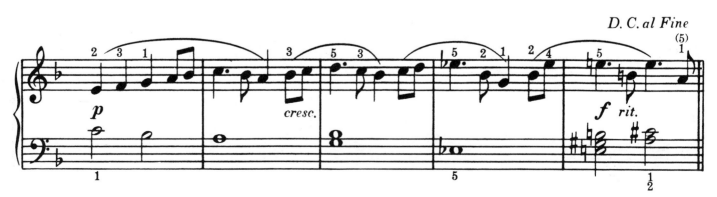

WP40

FUNERAL MARCH OF A MARIONETTE

(1st Theme)

CHARLES GOUNOD

arranged by James Bastien

Strict march tempo

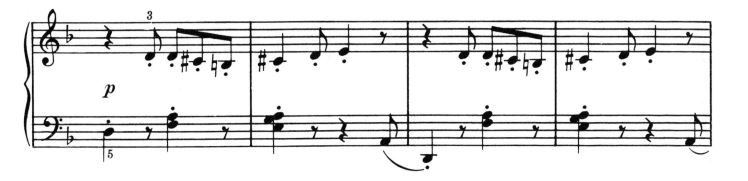

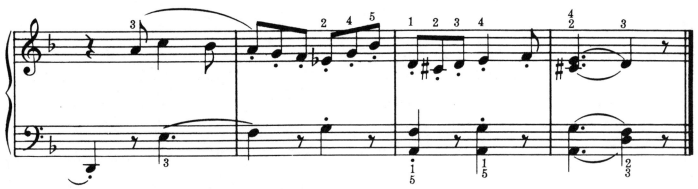

WP40

THE EVENING STAR

from the opera "Tannhäuser," Act II

RICHARD WAGNER

arranged by James Bastien

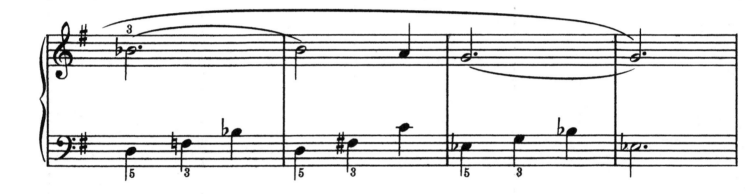

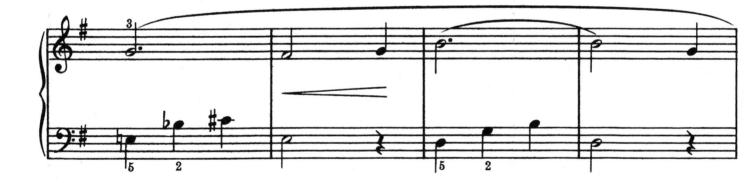

WP40

dim.

ANVIL CHORUS
from the opera "Il Trovatore," Act II

GIUSEPPE VERDI

arranged by James Bastien

Allegro maestoso

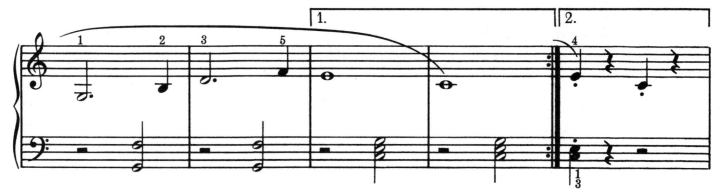

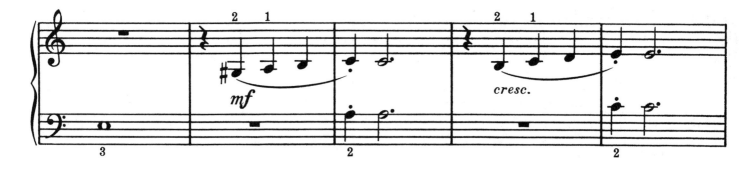

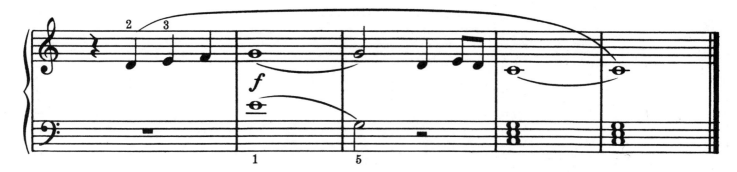

LIEBESTRAUM
from No. 3 for piano

FRANZ LISZT

arranged by James Bastien

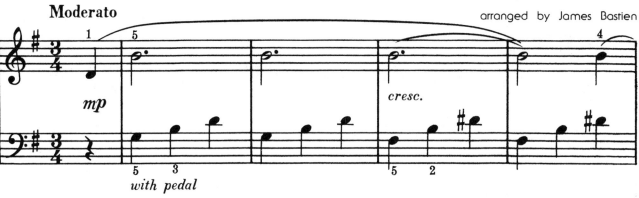

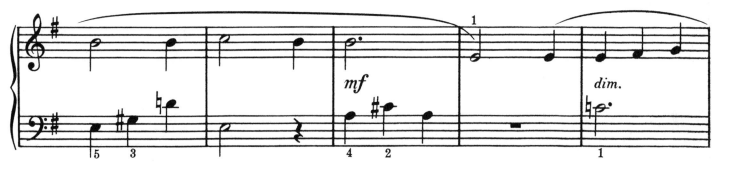

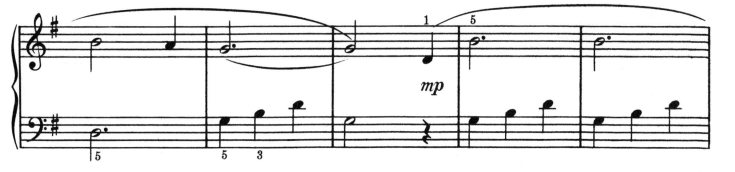

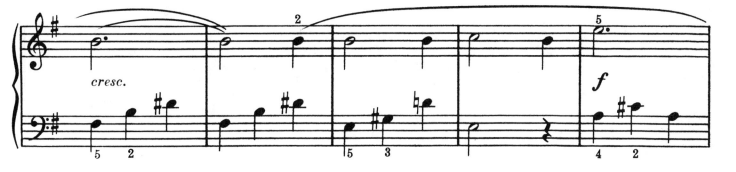

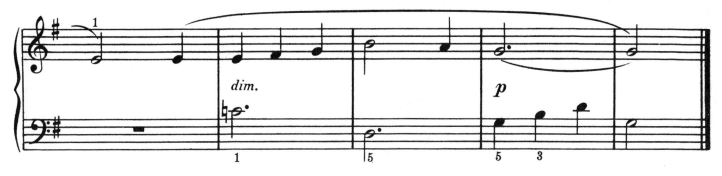

TORÉADOR SONG

from the opera "Carmen," Act II

GEORGES BIZET

arranged by James Bastien

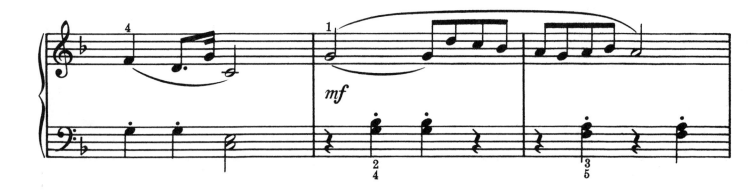

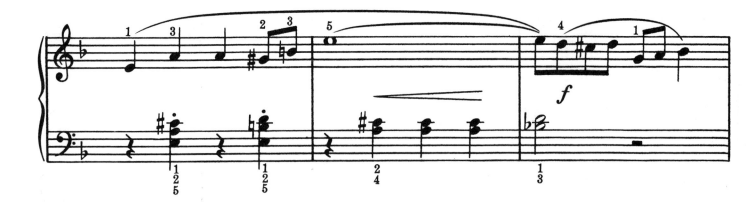

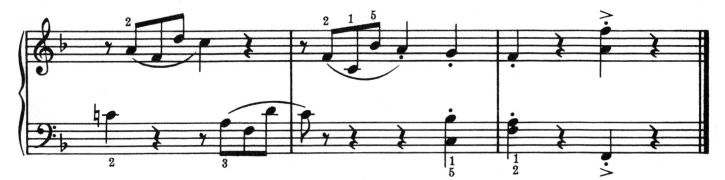

WP40

PILGRIM'S CHORUS

from the opera "Tannhäuser," Act II

RICHARD WAGNER

arranged by James Bastien

Andante

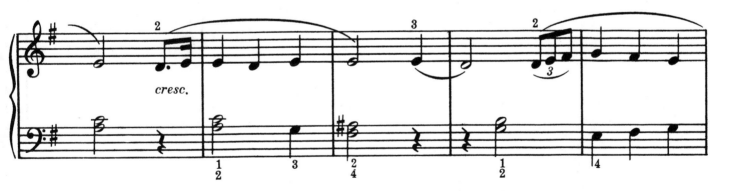

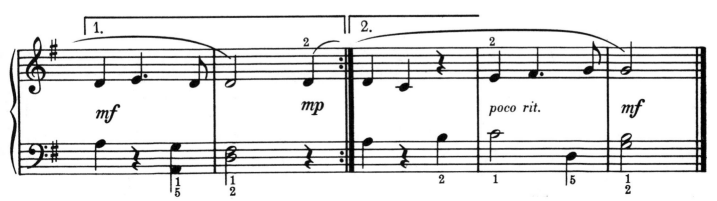

WP40

MY HEART AT THY SWEET VOICE

from the opera "Samson and Delilah," Act II

CAMILLE SAINT-SAËNS

arranged by James Bastien

Slowly and expressively

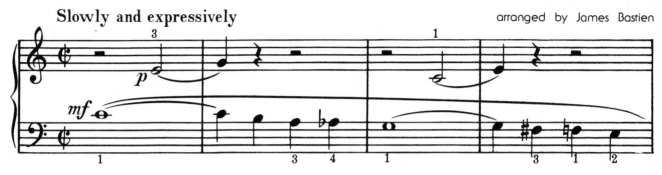

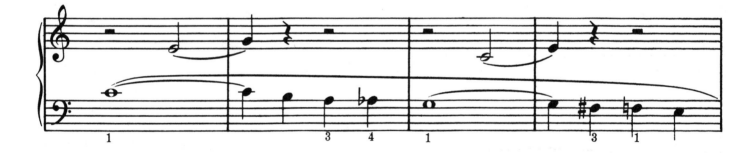

WP40

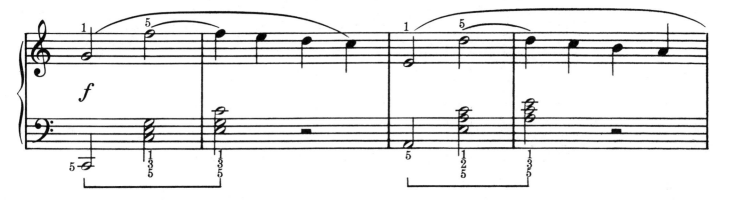

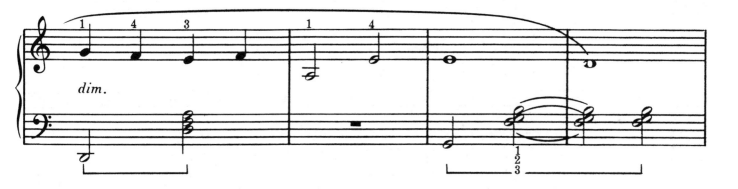

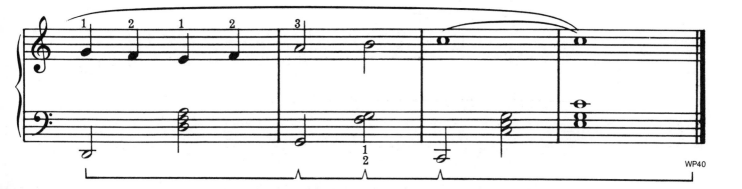

SYMPHONY NO. 5

from Op. 64
(Theme from 2nd Movement)

PETER ILYICH TCHAIKOVSKY

arranged by James Bastien

Andante cantabile

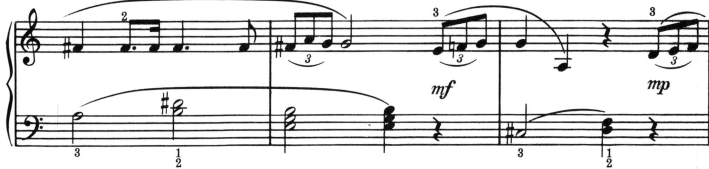

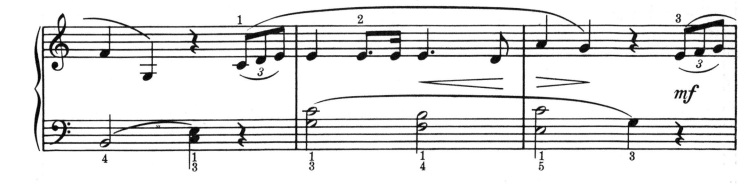

HEAVENLY AIDA

from the opera "Aida," Act I

GUISEPPE VERDI

arranged by James Bastien

Andante

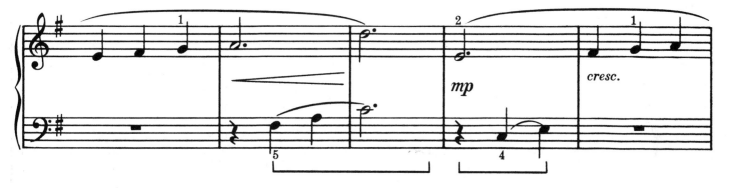

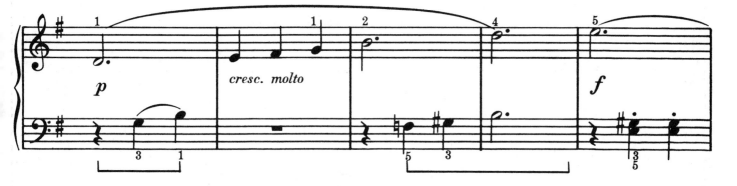

WP40

BRIDAL CHORUS

from the opera "Lohengrin," Act III

RICHARD WAGNER

arranged by James Bastien

Andante con moto

WP40

"UNFINISHED" SYMPHONY

from the Symphony No. 8
(Theme from 1st Movement)

FRANZ SCHUBERT

arranged by James Bastien

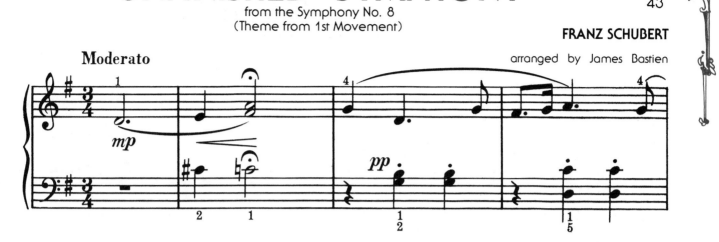

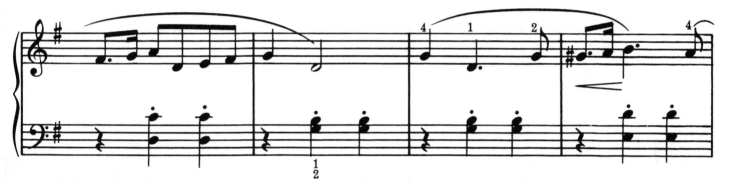

44

POLOVETZIAN DANCE
from the opera "Prince Igor," Act II

ALEXANDER BORODIN

arranged by James Bastien

Moderato

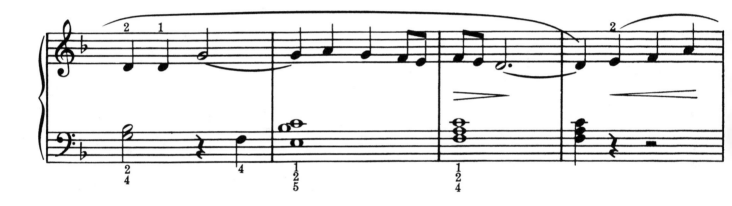

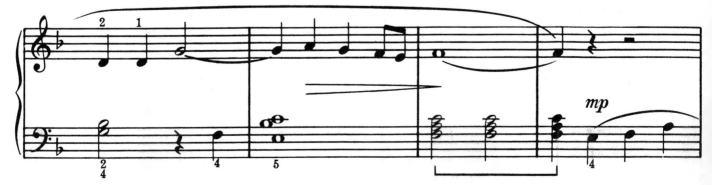

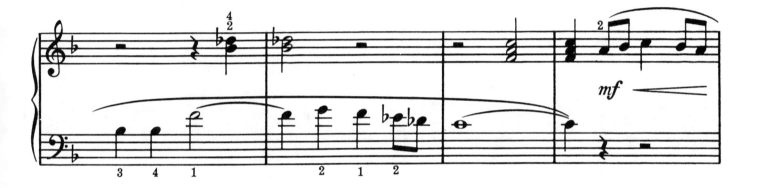

SONG OF INDIA

from the opera "Sadko," Act II

NICOLAI RIMSKY-KORSAKOFF

arranged by James Bastien

Andantino

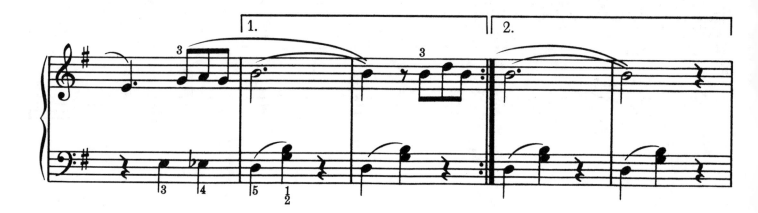

WP40

SERENADE

from "Schwanengesang" ("Swan Song") No. 4 for voice and piano

FRANZ SCHUBERT

arranged by James Bastien

Andante con moto

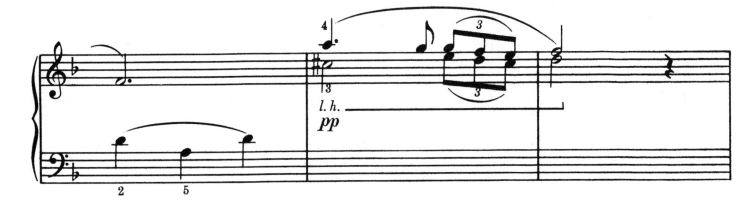

WP40

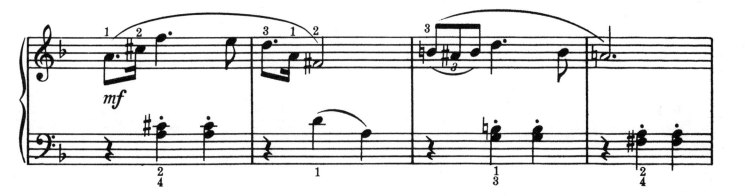

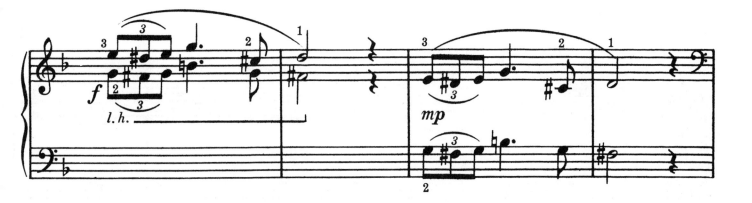

SCHEHERAZADE

from the Suite for Orchestra Op. 35
(Theme from 3rd Movement, "The Young Prince and the Princess")

NICOLAI RIMSKY-KORSAKOFF

arranged by James Bastien

Allegro moderato

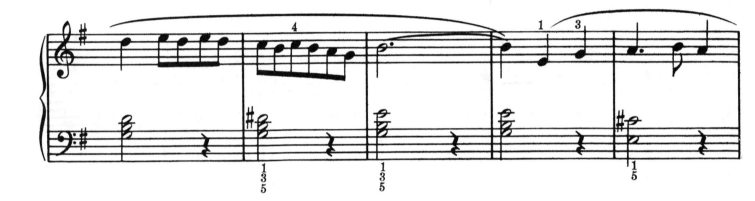

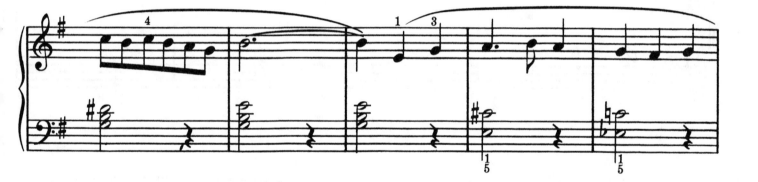

dim. e rit.

TALES FROM THE VIENNA WOODS

from the Concert Waltz Op. 325

JOHANN STRAUSS, JR.

arranged by James Bastien

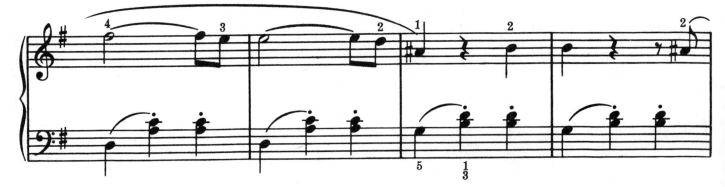

WP40

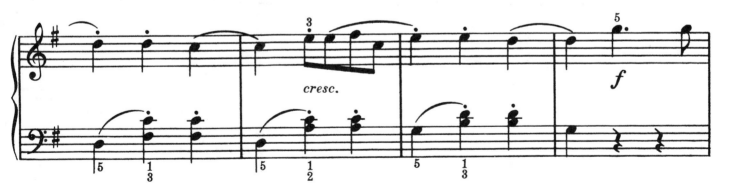

WP40

WALTZ
from the Waltz Op. 39, No. 15 for piano

JOHANNES BRAHMS

arranged by James Bastien

Moderato

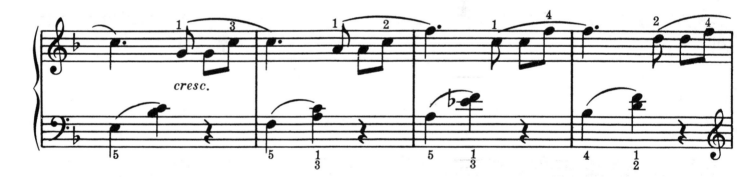

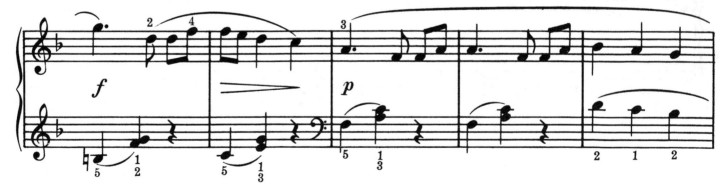

IN THE HALL OF THE MOUNTAIN KING

from "Peer Gynt Suite," No. 1, Op. 46
(Theme from 4th Movement)

EDVARD GRIEG

arranged by James Bastien

Allegro moderato

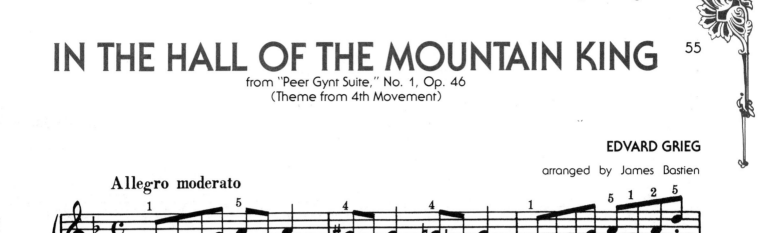

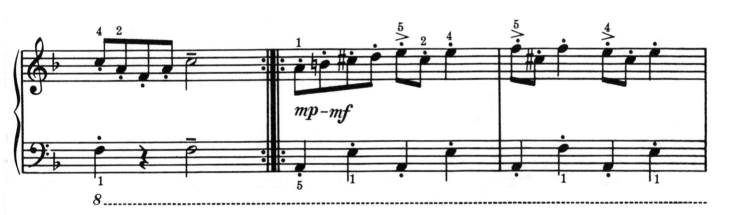

WP40

LAUGHING SONG

from the opera "Die Fledermaus," Act II

JOHANN STRAUSS, JR.

arranged by James Bastien

Tempo di valse

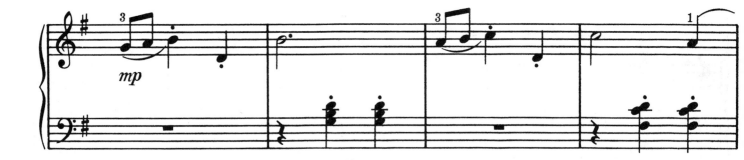

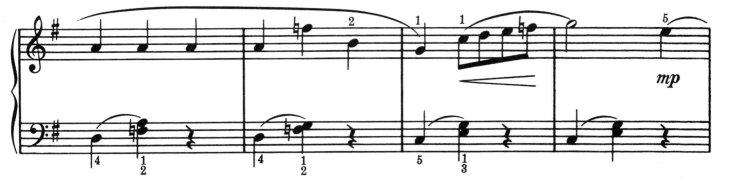

WP40

CONCERTO IN A MINOR

from the Concerto Op. 16 for piano and orchestra
(Theme from 1st Movement)

EDVARD GRIEG

arranged by James Bastien

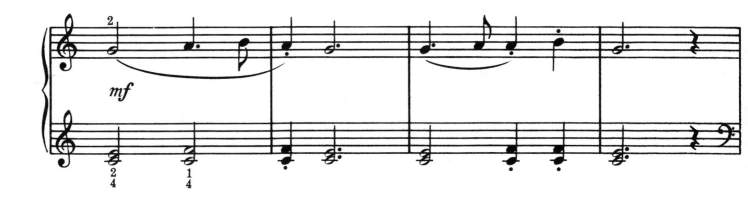

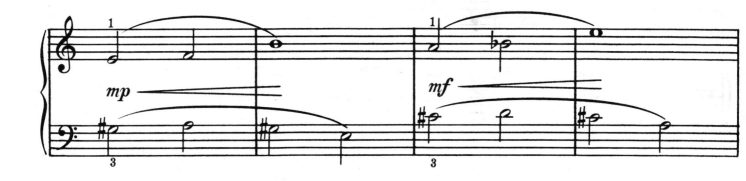

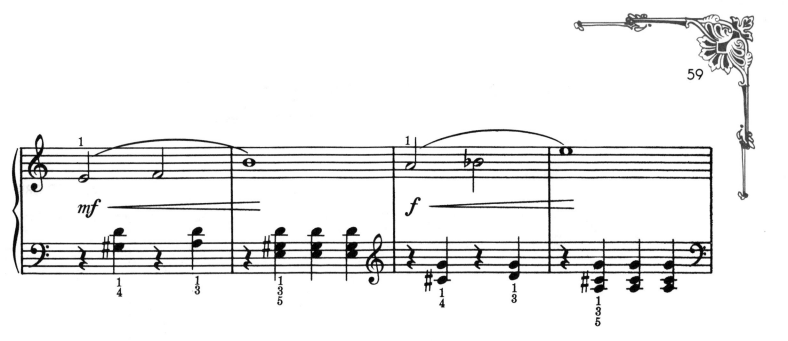

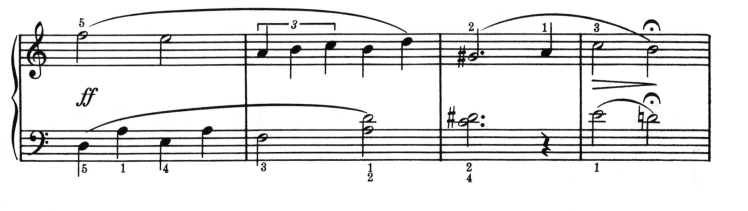

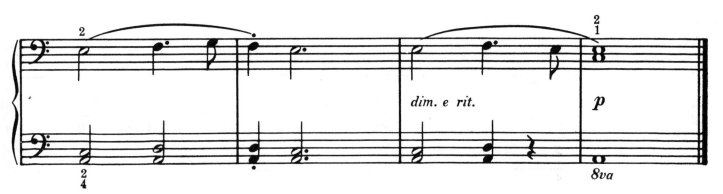

HUNGARIAN DANCE NO. 5

from the duet for piano

JOHANNES BRAHMS
arranged by James Bastien

Allegro moderato

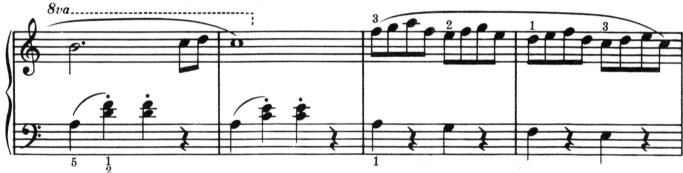

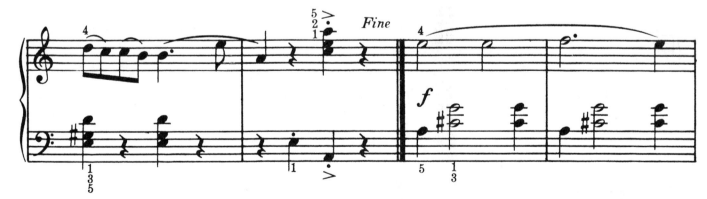

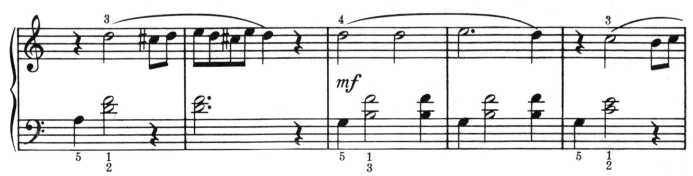

WP40

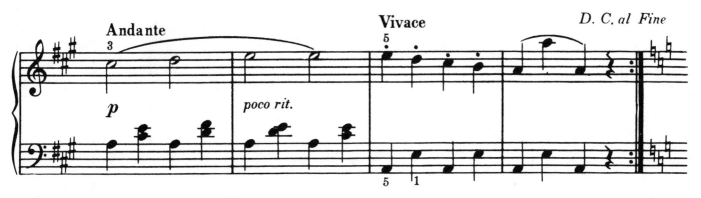

CONCERTO IN A MINOR

from the Concerto Op. 54 for piano and orchestra
(Theme from 1st Movement)

ROBERT SCHUMANN

arranged by James Bastien

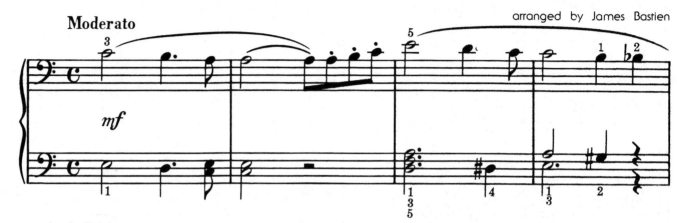

WP40

TRIUMPHAL MARCH
from the opera "Aida," Act II

GUISEPPE VERDI
arranged by James Bastien

CONCERTO NO. 1

from the Concerto No. 1, Op. 23 for piano and orchestra
(Theme from 1st Movement)

PETER ILYICH TCHAIKOVSKY

arranged by James Bastien

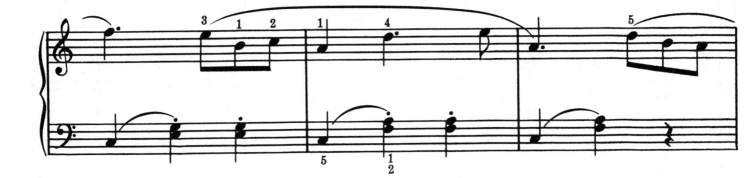

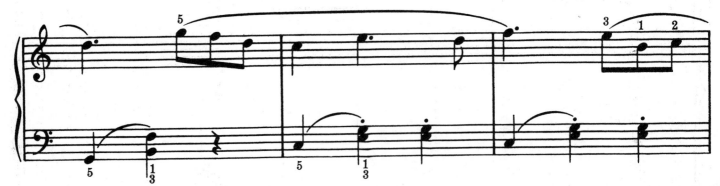

WP40

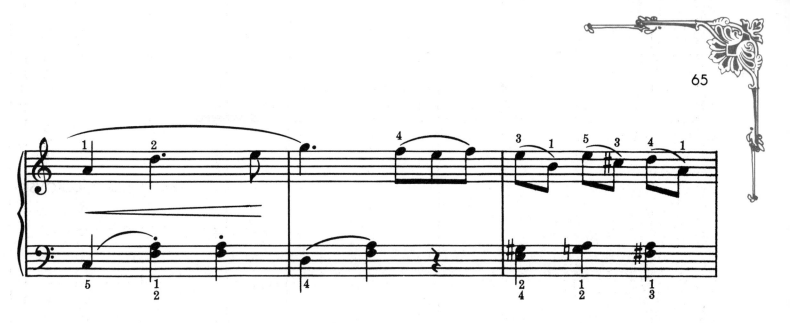

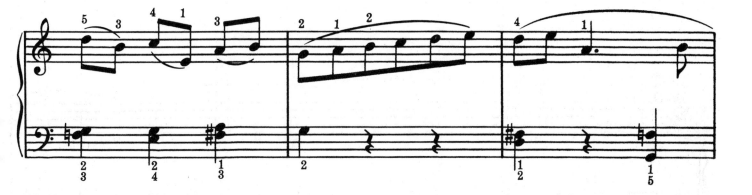

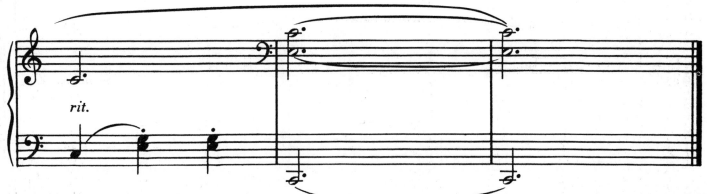

ROMEO AND JULIET

from the Overture-Fantasy
(3rd Theme)

PETER ILYICH TCHAIKOVSKY

arranged by James Bastien

Andante con moto

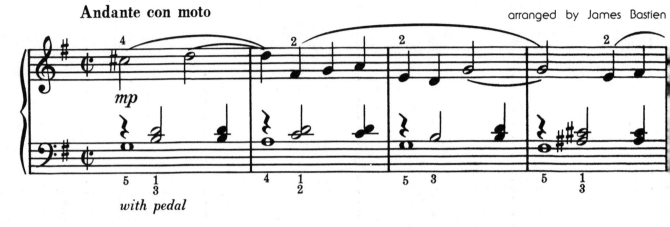

mp

with pedal

p

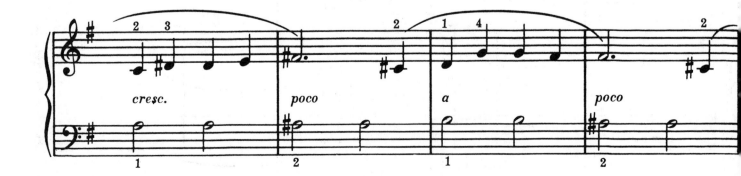

cresc.   *poco*   *a*   *poco*

WP4C

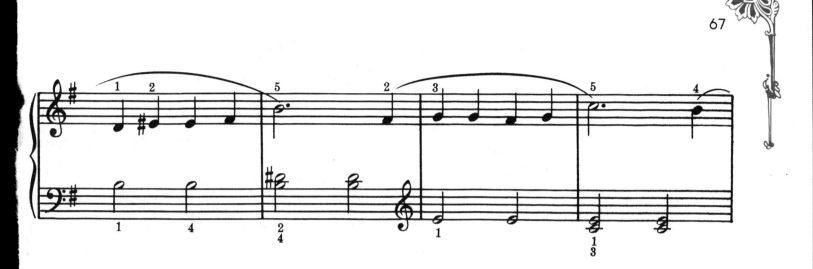

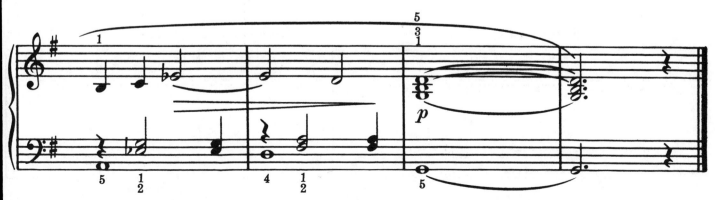

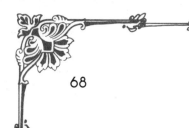

SYMPHONY NO. 5

from Op. 67
(Theme from 1st Movement)

LUDWIG VAN BEETHOVEN

arranged by James Bastien

Con spirito

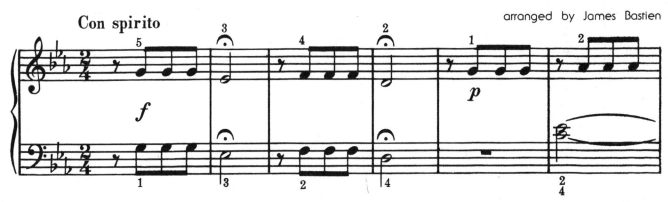

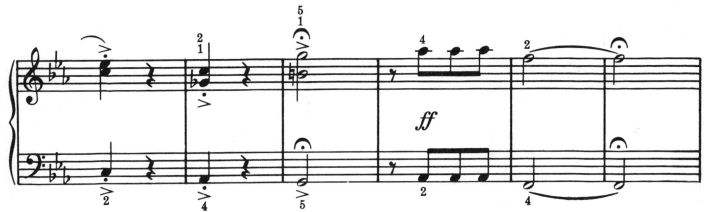

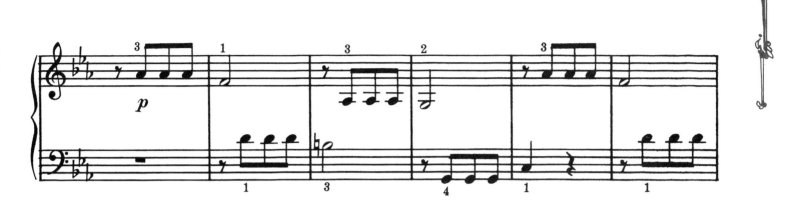

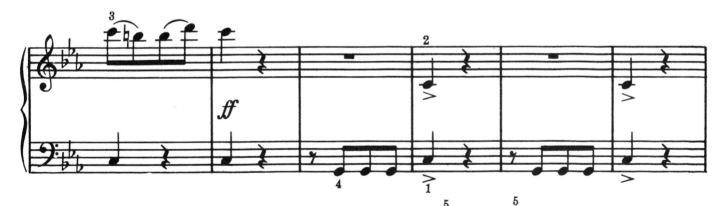

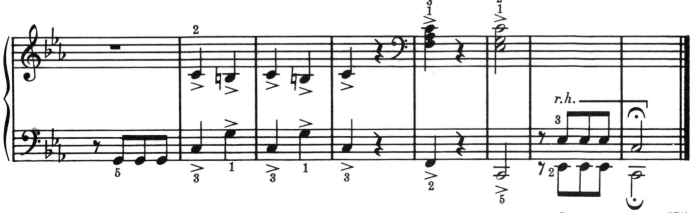

WP40

PETER AND THE WOLF

from Op. 67
(Peter's Theme)

SERGE PROKOFIEFF

arranged by James Bastien

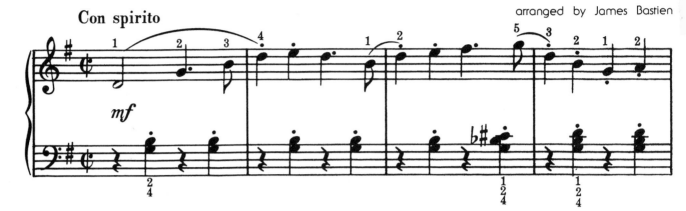

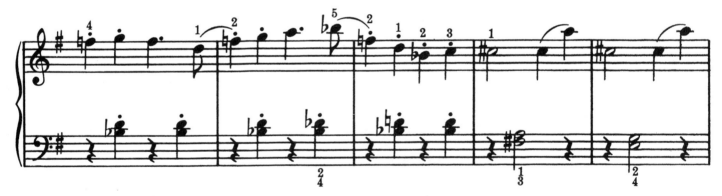

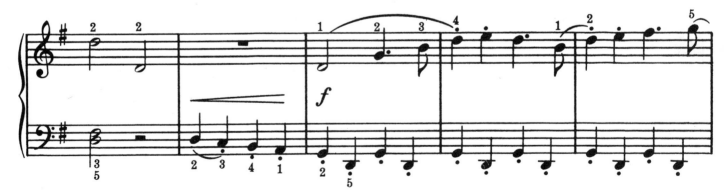

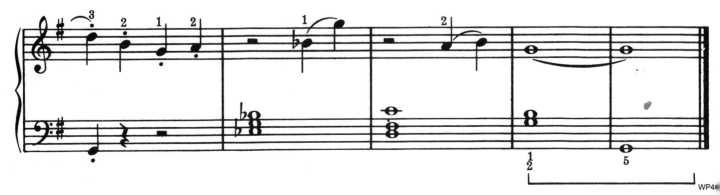

WP4

AIR FOR THE G STRING
from the Suite No. 3

JOHANN SEBASTIAN BACH

arranged by James Bastien

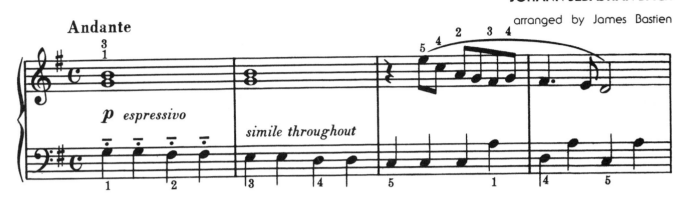

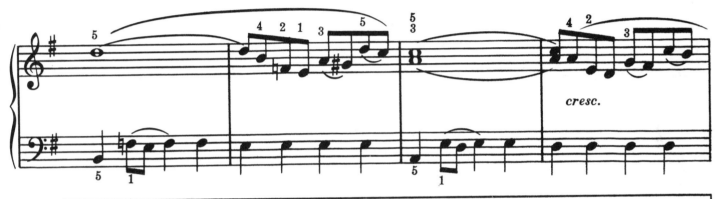

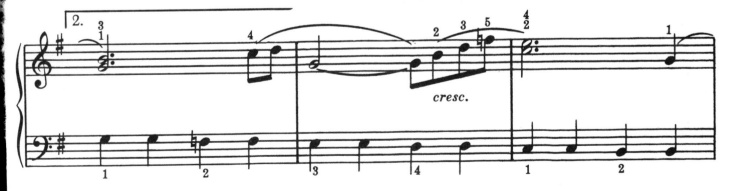

RUSSIAN DANCE

from "The Nutcracker Suite," Op. 71A

PETER ILYICH TCHAIKOVSKY

arranged by James Bastien

Vivace

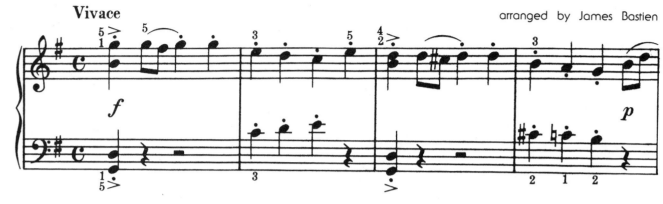